The Sure Mind

How Transformed Thinking Saved My Life

By: Evangelist Dorothea Ellen Royster

Dorothea Royster 2017©

All rights reserved. No part of this book may be reproduced in print, or by photostatic means, or in any other manner without the express permission of the publisher.

ISBN: 978-0-692-93971-0

Table of Contents

The Beginning to the End 1

Trouble Comes - "Oh God" 4

Stories Untold Until Now 15

The Voice 22

Meet the Method to my Problem 24

On my Way to Glory 28

Changed Mind, Stronger Woman 40

ACKNOWLEDGEMENTS 65

Chapter 1

The Beginning to the End

As I began thinking of how I would write my life story, I thought of all the people that made this possible. It's the ones I dedicated it to and many others. I'm thankful for the hurt; it made me grow by seeking a power unknown to me... until I met Jesus.

I lived in a foster home with loving parents, a grandmother also an older sister. We had a beautiful childhood. Much like a real home, we had rules that had to be followed. The love that was shown was beyond what I ever knew, a father at a table laughing; a mother looking with a smile on her face. Church on a regular basis, where we learned to know about God in a beautiful way, vacation Bible school, and vacations to the Cape. These were days and times that you just keep close to your heart and do not forget. This is what you see on TV; leave it to Beaver and Bill Cosby. Just wonderful, that's all I can say. There was also discipline, we had chores, but they were not hard. With the love I got, I cannot compare this to anything else. We were all happy and showed it.

Then to be pulled out of living in a situation that, you could not understand... fighting, cursing, drinking. Where was that stability that I once knew? We were young girls, ages eight to thirteen. Living with another father, we never knew our own dad. We also never heard any good stories concerning him. The ones I did hear were about him being a drug dealer and gangster. You can just fill in the rest for yourself. Lest I forget, I had another brother who died at a very early age. He is the reason why I'm able to write this story today.

Chapter 2
Trouble Comes - "Oh God"

Now, we were in a situation where the love was not the same. Sitting around the table was just like a picture in the frame. Mental and physical abuse was the game. We were called names that you wouldn't think a mother would call their own child. Left to me, this is what I felt; she means it, doesn't she? But it was on my mind for years. After leaving the foster home for this home, I cried "O God". I wanted to go home. Then my mother's husband mistreated and abused her. This is no way to live.

It was quiet for some time, but then he drank so much that he would talk so ugly to her. I thought to myself why would she want this in a husband. But his love was no love compared to my foster parents. I truly believe that my mother's childhood wasn't that good either. And now she had to deal with things that she did not discuss. She never had any kind words concerning my dad. I never understood that until I got older. As a young lady, she was still abusive to me and now I have a child. After my relationship ended, I came back home. I thought that I might be different now, but that was not the case. My stepfather was still the same. She took it and I still never understood. After going through my mistakes, I knew better but was still hurt, confused, and upset. I was raising a child on my own, still dealing with mind trials.

I just do not know what I'm doing, no love from my mother and not even from my step dad. But I loved my child with all my heart.

To sum it up, the relationship I had with my mother was not healthy for my son and I, so I decided to move away. This turned out to be a blessing, but I still heard the things my family talked about concerning the situation, that were not true. I felt like I always had to defend myself and no matter what, they always believed the lie instead of me. My son was too young and I didn't want him to be confused or caught in the maze. He was a bright child I and felt he didn't deserve that drama at all. I just wanted a normal life and a feeling that I was going on the right path. Having a child was not what I had wanted, but he was there and it was my job to protect him. His paternal grandmother was a great help and he spent time with her and the other members of his father's family. She also helped me get on the road to recovery. I got professional help with my issues and feelings.

At first, I was ashamed to let others find out, but it was helping me in so many ways. It was after a period of years before I realized that this was something I should have done a long time ago. Going for counseling allowed me to realize that it was not my fault, because my mother had issues before she even had children. They were within her childhood, and though she never spoke of them, I did hear many tales. I would ask her about the things that I heard and she would say it was none of my business or ask me who was I to question her life. It was heartbreaking and caused me to feel uncomfortable around her. The things that were told to me caused me to think that was the reason she acted the way she did. My foster mother never spoke bad about her at anytime, but would just say that my mom needed time to get her life in order. On the other hand, my mother spoke in ways that I would not want anyone to know, saying that my foster father did things to us. None of my foster family was ever mean or hateful, but just a loving family. Even my foster sister always cared and showed love to us. I hated to leave them because I knew we wouldn't ever be treated the same again. We were blessed, because you hear these days that other foster homes are cruel to the children and are only in it for the money. My son stayed with my foster family while I was in the hospital for my nerves. He still remembers them to this day as sweet loving people.

At times, my son would stay with his grandmother on father's side so I could get my thoughts together. During those times, I was depressed and just didn't know how to feel so I would call her and ask could Roger come to her house and stay a while. I felt like I could not give him the attention that a mother should, but I thank God for her and how she has been there to help me out. It was hard for him to understand why I was so unhappy, while at the same time was trying to make his life the best ever. He was a smart boy and as cute as ever in my eyesight. I didn't want his life to be like mine and for him not to know his father, so they spent time together on vacations in the summer and during holidays. This made me happy. My son loved visiting his dad and his family so he was happy being there.

At times, it was just my son and I. We would go to the park to play games, and he liked to cook. It was hard being a single parent, but I did the best that I could. I wished I had gotten married. My foster mother told me that you should get married before having children. I looked for love in all the wrong places. I loved my son's father and I believe that he loved me at one time. We were very young when we met and I thought he was "the cat's meow", so to speak. It didn't work out and home I went, to live with my mother, which was hell on wheels. I always stayed in the house, never going out. I was feeling sorry for myself and telling myself I would never have another child. My mom was always sweet to Roger. One day he came home with a scuff on his shoe and she hit him and I thought it was too hard. I thought that it was wrong for her to hit him that hard and put him in a dark room. That's when I decided the living situation wasn't working out because my mom was being mean to Roger and abusing him. I moved out, it was the best thing to do. When I did, my mom would not come visit me much at all, but when she did she would let me know that she was just coming to see her grandson. She always made fun of how I fixed up my apartment. She would say things like she didn't like the curtain in my room or just anything to hurt my feelings, and it worked. I would cry for half the night and say to myself, "here we go again." Nothing I did good was ever good enough for her. At times I just wanted to tell her that at least I was taking care of my own, but I wouldn't hurt her like she hurt me. This went on for years, where she would say things about my hair, clothes or anything that would hurt me, but never did the same to my sisters and brother. I think she took pleasure in hurting others, including her own children. How could I be a young women feeling, "if your mother doesn't have feelings for you, so why would others?" It was a crazy situation and very hurtful. It didn't make me feel good about myself at all. Sometimes I didn't know what to think of myself, my life or anything else.

From an early age, my mind was good. It was free and happy and I believe this was the doing of my foster family, but things changed when I returned to my mother's. I was smart mouthed at times and talked back to her and others, which was not right. During my teenage years I went out and partied with family and friends, and after while I started drinking and doing other things I knew I had no business doing at all. I was just a young girl looking for love and a happy life. I dated somewhat, but soon found out that guys were wanting me to have sex. I was a virgin until I was eighteen. That was a period in my life that changed everything. When I got pregnant, I didn't know anything about being a mother and was so scared and very alone. My mother was angry when I told her and she told me that I needed to get married. Neither my child's father nor myself were ready for marriage, never mind being parents. I loved him very much but we were two young people with a child. We didn't last long as a couple but remained friends somewhat.

How could I let him go through what I did? But my mother proved to be abusive to him. As I said before, he had messed up a pair of school shoes, mother spanked him and left him alone in a dark room. To know that was a straw that broke my back. He does not deserve such a punishment. Now it's time to move on. Just my son and I.

At times, my thoughts were, "when did this happen to her? Why would you do this to your grandchild that you said you loved?" Many tears rolling from my eyes, holding him close, wondering why. I'm grown and she still speaks out of term to me. And I'm still a mess with other relationships. I have no wonder why they were no good at all.

I began writing poems at the age of sixteen. I started with love letters for friends at school and I thought I did well, but it was my pass to feel a release when things at home were a mess. I would think of flowing streams and mountain tops. No one ever knew how I felt about writing. But I had to hear glass breaking to call the police. These are not my kids. That shocked my core. I wrote more to hide my feelings on paper.

Being a mother at nineteen was not easy. Looking for love all in the wrong places, but I brought him here. And he did not ask me to come. I had to try to do things right, but that was another story itself. I was a good mother, and I thought he had the best of everything... dressed well, even for Pre-K. He received the best dressed one year. I tried showing him love, but how do you give it when you don't know how or don't even know what it is? All I could do was think of what my foster parents did for me. He was a bright child and I wanted him to have love. You could read about it but a book does not have instructions on how and when to give it. I believe it must be in you to come out.

That is when I started to realize that my mother didn't know how to love and be loved. And she was not the type that should have had children. I told her that and she was very upset with me. But the truth is the truth and it will set you free. She was not loved in her marriage and I saw that. She was not a loving mother either. Her way of love was to buy it but there isn't a price that anyone could ever pay for love. It was so sad to see her at times. And to know that I was going to be put down or be talked about behind my back, she destroyed a lot of me. And I wonder how I will ever recover and be the mother I need to be. But the person I need to be first is me. It caused me to accept and do things that I would not do. I need help just for my mind right. Counseling helped for a while and years that led me to realize a pill to wake up, walk around, and then go to bed was not going to work. Losing my hair and skin was a mess and I had to stop. I tried many drugs and alcohol; they didn't bring love back to my broken heart, my empty bed and purse. I needed something that would make me love my child. I wondered what that could be and I searched and searched until I couldn't find anything that made me feel good about myself. See, my mother would say that I would never look as good as her other daughter. She said that I should have been a boy after coming home with a short haircut that she didn't even approve of. She knew how to cut you without a knife and still make you bleed. My sisters and brother didn't know how they affected me either. See I didn't feel as smart as they were; they have degrees. My mother's favorite statement towards me was that I was a glorified butt washer. I'm a certified nursing assistant, but if that makes me a butt washer, to God be the glory. Someone has to do it and I'm that person. She did not approve of me at all. See, I had a child out of wedlock. My mother had five, but to her I was the worst of her daughters. She told me that when I told her I was pregnant. "Not you, I expected the others." But sex at times was a way of finding love, only to be hurt again.

"They said it couldn't be done...."

Chapter 3
Stories Untold Until Now

I lived in a secret place for many years. Others would not believe me if I told them the things I had to endure, but you must realize this is because we were a dysfunctional family. What went on at home, you kept at home. If it did get out, you knew a beating would happen. You better not tell a soul, even my own soul. I did not know if I had one or what and who was in control. There were so many family secrets, even until this day. Even the ones I know are the truth aren't talked about. Not knowing that living a lie can cause someone to die and the ones that could free you may cause some to want to hide. I used to be ashamed when I used to hear things my mother didn't know that others did tell me. Until I read an article in the newspaper about how she lost her two-year-old son and why I had to go to a foster home. She enjoyed the streets better than her five children. She left one in the apartment and he fell to his death.

This, as I said before, is the reason I can write this. He saved our lives when this occurred. The police thought we were my mom's brothers and sisters instead of her children. When you find love in the wrong places, this is what happens. It's not anything she could talk about. And I had a hard time believing this is what she did. But now I know why and it's no secret that her parents didn't know either. It's so sad to me that she had to die of un-forgiveness. I crossed her over to salvation, but at times when she, even in death, was hateful and mean. She had not forgiven the ones who hurt her and this is how cancer formed. I thank God every day for the lessons I did learn from her and the ones I'd rather not share. Before all of the news was given to me, I had dreams and would share them with others that said that I would be ok and that I should go back to sleep. Not knowing that they were about his death and how it occurred. But now my dreams are of my life and how God is preparing me for greatness. And other times, my dreams are used to warn people and I can tell them to be careful.

At first, I was ashamed to let others find out, but it was helping me in so many ways. It was after a period of years before I realized that this was something I should have done a long time ago. Going for counseling allowed me to realize that it was not my fault, because my mother had issues before she even had children. They were within her childhood, and though she never spoke of them, I did hear many tales. I would ask her about the things that I heard and she would say it was none of my business or ask me who was I to question her life. It was heartbreaking and caused me to feel uncomfortable around her. The things that were told to me caused me to think that was the reason she acted the way she did. My foster mother never spoke bad about her at anytime, but would just say that my mom needed time to get her life in order. On the other hand, my mother spoke in ways that I would not want anyone to know, saying that my foster father did things to us. None of my foster family was ever mean or hateful, but just a loving family. Even my foster sister always cared and showed love to us. I hated to leave them because I knew we wouldn't ever be treated the same again. We were blessed, because you hear these days that other foster homes are cruel to the children and are only in it for the money. My son stayed with my foster family while I was in the hospital for my nerves. He still remembers them to this day as sweet loving people.

At times, my son would stay with his grandmother on father's side so I could get my thoughts together. During those times, I was depressed and just didn't know how to feel so I would call her and ask could Roger come to her house and stay a while. I felt like I could not give him the attention that a mother should, but I thank God for her and how she has been there to help me out. It was hard for him to understand why I was so unhappy, while at the same time was trying to make his life the best ever. He was a smart boy and as cute as ever in my eyesight. I didn't want his life to be like mine and for him not to know his father, so they spent time together on vacations, in the summer and during holidays. This made me happy. My son loved visiting his dad and his family so he was happy being there.

At times, it was just my son and I. We would go to the park to play games, and he liked to cook. It was hard being a single parent, but I did the best that I could. I wished I had gotten married. My foster mother told me that you should get married before having children. I looked for love in all the wrong places. I loved my son's father and I believe that he loved me at one time. We were very young when we met and I thought he was "the cat's meow", so to speak. It didn't work out and home I went, to live with my mother, which was hell on wheels. I always stayed in the house, never going out. I was feeling sorry for myself and telling myself I would never have another child. To sum it up, the relationship I had with my mother was not healthy for my son and I, so I decided to move away. This turned out to be a blessing, but I still heard the things my family talked about concerning the situation, that were not true. I felt like I always had to defend myself and no matter what, they always believed the lie instead of me. My son was too young and I didn't want him to be confused or caught in the maze. He was a bright child and I felt he didn't deserve that drama at all. I just wanted a normal life and a feeling that I was going on the right path. Having a child was not what I had wanted, but he was there and it was my job to protect him. His paternal grandmother was a great help and he spent time with her and the other members of his father's family. She also helped me get on the road to recovery. I got professional help with my issues and feelings.

I moved out; it was the best thing to do. When I did, my mom would not come visit me much at all, but when she did she would let me know that she was just coming to see her grandson. She always made fun of how I fixed up my apartment. She would say things like she didn't like the curtain in my room or just anything to hurt my feelings, and it worked. I would cry for half the night and say to myself, "here we go again." Nothing I did good was ever *good enough* for her. At times I just wanted to tell her that at least I was taking care of my own, but I wouldn't hurt her like she hurt me. This went on for years, where she would say things about my hair, clothes or anything that would hurt me, but never did the same to my sisters and brother. I think she took pleasure in hurting others, including her own children. How could I be a young woman feeling, "if your mother doesn't have feelings for you, why would others?" It was a crazy situation and very hurtful. It didn't make me feel good about myself at all. Sometimes I didn't know what to think of myself, my life or anything else.

From an early age, my mind was good. It was free and happy and I believe this was the doing of my foster family, but things changed when I returned to my mother's. I was smart mouthed at times and talked back to her and others, which was not right. During my teenage years I went out and partied with family and friends, and after while I started drinking and doing other things I knew I had no business doing at all. I was just a young girl looking for love and a happy life. I dated somewhat, but soon found out that guys were wanting me to have sex. I was a virgin until I was eighteen. That was a period in my life that changed everything. When I got pregnant, I didn't know anything about being a mother and was so scared and very alone. My mother was angry when I told her and she told me that I needed to get married. Neither me or my child's father were ready for marriage, much less being parents. I loved him very much but we were two young people with a child. We didn't last long as a couple but remained friends somewhat.

Chapter 4
The Voice

Family members and older ones were no angels at all. They pretended to live right but I saw through that too. The way they answered a question when asked... the anger that came from their voices told more than I had liked to see. That same spirit fell on me. Yes, I was mean and I was hateful too. I thought it was okay; I always used to hear, "she is just like her mother". Whether they knew it or not, I hated to hear that. I never wanted to be like her, to make someone feel so bad inside was not me. But to live it was worse than anyone could ever imagine. And I looked just like my dad who I never knew. The stories about him would keep me wide awake. A change had to come about. It was not hard to do. Inside I was a lamb, just wondering how to get out. I was not treated as well as the others and that had to change too. I had to forgive them, forgive myself and leave it at the feet of Jesus.

The words I wanted to hear were" I love you." My mother did not express her love in ways that I could see. We never did anything that I could remember as good or fun. The things I used to hear are "You are stupid", "Dumb Niggers", "All you are doing is taking someone else's place", "You are not like your sister. She is pretty and she is also smart. You look like a little boy. You will never be as pretty as my other daughters and do not forget that!" So that made me to question how I looked. Still to this day, I question it. We can cause this to be a problem in our children's lives later on. They will need constant reassurance in this area. The words we speak to them can cause major harm, anger, and so much misery.

Chapter 5
Meet the Method to my Problem

I could have been a single mother of two, but the child I have now is the one I kept. The other one that would have been was from a life that I'll never forget. I did not love the father and sometimes wonder about the other child I could have had. I was too afraid then to see what things could have been. What would she have looked like?

My foster mother would call me her religious daughter. At nine, I was carrying a Bible and could quote scriptures too. I would take it to the park and read it. I didn't know how much it would play such a big part in my life. My first and favorite was "Forgive them lord. They know not what they do." I knew that they were laughing at me. They thought it was all a joke, but it wasn't. It was time to know what the scriptures meant and how to apply it to my life.

I needed someone to love and to talk to... someone that would understand and believe in me. Where was I going to find this person? Even after hanging out on a

Saturday night in the pew, way in the back so no one could see me.

I talked to so many people about Jesus, God, Christ. The love he had. His death was what attracted me. To die for someone was the most ultimate sacrifice that I had ever heard about. Then to know that he had never lied or sinned at all. I had to sit down and ponder over these facts. I wanted to know how to get to know him; he could take the place of my parents that really didn't love me. They did not know how to love themselves so how could they love me?

I was not a perfect parent either. I had my fair share. I hung in the streets, slept with guys that were not worth the pain or shame that I had to live with after they were gone. I loved my son's father but he did not really know that. He was a hitter and a name caller too. So, I was right back where I left off. I was just a messed-up mind. Just a wreck. I heard a voice that said I should die. Tried it. God had me close so I would not die. My mother didn't think much of me. She would call her mother and say that it didn't feel right with me being there. Something was wrong but she would say that she heard that before. I needed help. There was an angel, a woman that had helped me like my mother should have. To this day, she is very important in ways she may never know. But in my heart, it is still a story untold. The lord replaced my mother and father in ways that others just do not know. They say he was a ram in a bush. It's true. The mothers (they know who they are) and the fathers have gone on, but it blesses my soul to be called daughter by their friends and to be treated like a daughter was unbelievable. My foster mother gave me my start. She talked to me as a mother should and though she punished me when I needed to be, she hugged and loved me too. My foster dad made me laugh when I sneezed because he would say my brain was dust. That home was like no other.

Now in the world of sex, drugs, and parties, I was hanging out like I knew it all. But it was time to get out of the streets, living that lifestyle before I ended up dead in an early grave. I liked hanging out late and doing clubs, having a good time. Ruff necks seemed to be the thing then, but to tell the truth, what women think today is not for me. I did know that guys thought I was fine back then but they also thought I was mean. I did not care what they thought at that time, but later on, I wanted someone to love more than just one week or a month, but for a lifetime love. My cousin used to say, "You're too mean. Why are you like that?" It was a way to not get hurt. I realized that all I was doing was running them away for some other girl to have. Another change had to come. No more clubbing, no more fun and bed hopping.

I decided I could no longer wait. I needed this love every day, every hour, and every second. Oh lord! Please tell me how to reach you. We were at church and my cousin was singing. I couldn't keep still, but I didn't know why. I wanted to run and jump. My spirit was so high and I still didn't get what was happening. Now I know the Lord had touched me and I was having a feeling that I would never forget. It's hard to describe. Only to the ones that know what the anointing of God is like on you. Then I wanted to tell my family but how could I? And when I do explain things that have happened, they would just laugh, but it's ok. To have the degree I have now isn't what I need to master Jesus. To master Jesus is a lifetime degree. So I'll be in the Bible until he comes. I know that he is not returning for the PHD, BSN or Master. Do not bother to stand in his line. His return is for the ones like me: hurt, used, abused, downtrodden, hated, unloved, and casted down.

Chapter 6

On my Way to Glory

The reason why I knew that God was my last hope is that no matter what I tried, nothing was working. I was still frustrated, confused and unhappy, I needed a way out. I felt like prayer was the key to many things that I couldn't tell others without getting upset, crying or hurting them as they had hurt me. Enough is enough! I wanted to forgive and be forgiven if that was at all possible. It seemed like I asked God for his forgiveness every time I went into prayer. I found scriptures that spoke on forgiveness and got several books on it as well. Charles Stanley had a good one on forgiveness with a workbook which was very helpful. I must say that the process is not something that could be done overnight. It took months of pain and conviction too. I know I played a huge part in the time it took because I would rehearse over and over what this person said and what that person did. That was not "getting over it" at all. It was just going around and around in a never ending cycle. This was the point where I had to learn to forgive myself and it was the hardest of all. Every day I prayed, "Lord, take it away," because it was making me feel sick inside and unable to eat and sleep. There were days and even weeks of this and they were horrible. I said to myself, "Who lives a life like this?....THIS IS NOT LIVING AT ALL."

All the hurt took me to a place outside of church to realize one thing. It was not about me or you, but about Christ. What I needed from him and what he needed me to do. Laying on my face, facing the truth, not about you, but me, standing in the need of prayer. It's me Lord. This time, I, Dorothea, care to be different and free of my past. I know with him, I will last. And now he is my future and he will not pass me by. So, I said before my glory cloud, "Lord please form over me and mine". I know that this cloud I'm on now, I once tried to run from. But all the pain pushed me so hard and I love this type of glory cloud. I learned that I'm good enough for Jesus, if not anyone else. It's all good. It's all God and his glory. I'll never have to hide.

After a six month period, I was doing better, and was still seeking counsel, which helped too. I felt better and liked myself a little at the time. The biggest part was letting others know that I forgave them for hurting me while they were trying to go back and re-visit the past and I was trying to move on. I did move on and it was a journey that I wouldn't take again. I had to just leave people and memories alone at times, in order to live a life of peace. At times, I wished I was closer to those people who caused the hurt, but I have tried it and found that it was not a place for me to go back to. They know how I am and think they know my life now. It is so much better with the Lord and I don't feel like trading this world I have with him for theirs. There is just something about going in prayer for a situation you cannot bear and knowing that God knew what to do before you even asked him what to do. Being active in church helps and talking with those who understand that, where you are is not where everyone else is. It also helps to know that my life is not taken lightly because the Lord sees and knows.

My desire to feel good about myself was a need. I recall how as a young girl I would ask my sisters how things looked on me and things like that. It took years before I realized that I am not bad looking. I needed confidence but, where ever would I get it? The word of God spoke of "my BELOVED" and those words stuck out to me and I repeated them. "The Apple of My Eye" and "I Love you with an everlasting love", were all key words to me. I never told anyone, but these words from someone who I could not see made me feel special that someone could feel this way about me.

It was like medicine for my hurt and confused soul. My foster mother would call us her "rubies" so all that I heard in Sunday school came into view.

I was an adult but almost like a baby to receive these words after hearing things like, "You are ugly. . . You don't even know how to dress… No one wants you." I had to get this out of my mind. I read the Bible more. It was my life line to peace and joy again. I really became interested in the Word of God and started buying books on religious things that could help me. I attended church more and also the events in church where I could get involved. I didn't know that people at church were hurting too, and therefore I was in the right place for the right reason. I thought it was supposed to start at home, but for me that wasn't so. My grandmother had sat on the front row at church and was the head missionary, but she wasn't happy all the time. I also saw so many people in my family hurting. It wasn't just me, but I felt like this was my struggle and not theirs. We were as messed up as any other family, I just didn't see or know about other people's at the time. My uncles drank pretty heavy. Others of my family members did "their thing" to cope and though I saw that happening, I didn't know that they had issues too. I asked questions and sometimes got answers I just couldn't believe or did not want to hear and believe.

"And Jesus loves the little children. Yellow, black, and white. They are all precious in his sight….."

My saving grace was at church being around strong-willed people and never trying to go back to the hurt or that old stuff again. I received Jesus Christ for real (this time) in 1996. Before this, I would play church, but now it lives in me really strong. Yes, I have dealt with "church hurt" that made me realize that when you have a calling on your life, not everyone is going to tell you "baby, you are anointed." They just ain't going to tell you, but I knew I had something when I would know things about people when I first met them, before they told me. I discovered that I have the gift of discernment. Years went on and I asked God for tongues. At first I didn't know what they were, but I am glad that I can now speak in my heavenly language. Yes, the Word of God was my way to deal with things better. My grandson died at the age of seventeen and that someone pushed me over the edge. I had just told him that I knew he was doing something that he had no business doing. I talked to him on a Sunday and that next Monday he was dead. I told my son all about the car that was involved and what had happened because I had a vision of it in a dream. That was just a little bit of what God had given me in this gift, but it shocked my son. God speaks to me through dreams and through other people. I try to encourage others to know that if God loves you, then you are loved. One day while standing in the window, it was a voice saying "I Love You" and I thought it was my son, but now I know it was the voice of God. That was another turning point in my life because I knew I could move on from there.

My mother never really knew that I was sold out for the Lord. She use to call me a "holy roller", but that didn't bother me. I wonder if she had a relationship with God at all. How do you go to church for all those years and not get close to God at all? A "pew warmer" is what I use to say, but I can say that I lead her to salvation before she died and I felt that was my gift to her in God. I hope to see my family saved and living for God. He said in his Word that he will do it. If I die before it happens, I know it will still come to pass.

The mind of Christ must be sure. It is with our mind that we serve him. Kings of Kings, Lords of Lords. Without deliverance, which is not once but 365 days; a year; 24/7. Then you do not go right to heaven. You must get in a church where the word is being preached. Taught out of the pulpit under the anointing of Christ. Be obedient to the leadership of those who have rule over you. Be faithful in your giving and the things of God.

Found my hope in a God I couldn't see.
Peace of mind was all I wanted…
..To know love and to be loved and show love
Words I couldn't speak laid at his feet
Hope for a better tomorrow was my prayer.
Never knew love could be like this.
Learn how to pray through the hurt and shame.

*You are never too old to set another goal
or to dream a new dream.*

C.S. Lewis

"With God, all things are possible."
Luke 1:37

"Refuse to quit."

Chapter 7
Changed Mind, Stronger Woman

My brother and sisters never knew how they had made me feel. At times they never invited me with them and most of the time I had to find out about the things they were doing from someone else outside of the family. I felt like I never fitted in, but they kept on saying, "yes you do." They really didn't pay much attention to me. The only time they would was when I would address them first or if I was acknowledged by others first. Otherwise, they would say, "hush, don't bother me with that." I sometimes had emotional problems, thinking about how I was treated by my family members. Many times, I would stay to myself and try to deal with it on my own or talk to my spiritual mother. We would pray and she would tell me how to deal with it. It was like a nightmare I just couldn't get over. No one would want to listen when I wanted to talk about how I felt.

Family secrets was exactly what they were...never to be mentioned at all. My brother moved away and came back to visit from time to time, mostly holidays and special occasions. Then he became a social worker and I was proud of him, but we still didn't talk about things too much at all. My older sister and I didn't get along well at all. She just had ways about her that I couldn't deal with. It's the same today, though she had cancer and I thought that might draw us closer. It did, but only for a short time. My baby sister was always caught in the middle of our arguments and I didn't feel it was fair to her. I just cut off contact with them to avoid the fights and lies that were being told. She moved to Germany to teach and then I was just left there with my problems, but felt that they would go away. I missed her so much at times. She was the peacemaker of all of us.

After my mother's death I thought we would get along better, but that did not happen. It didn't happen when she was alive, of course, but partly because my mom was the one that would keep mess going between us, which I thought was a very sick situation. I never understood how she would lie to one telling them something that was never said and when asked about it, she would deny it. My son was her only grandchild and he would ask me why she was like that. I never had the answers for him. I just thought to myself that she was evil and it hurt me to know that. Despite all that, she loved him and he loved her. She would always say how handsome he was and he could do no wrong in her eyes. Whenever I would tell him that he needed to behave, she would say I was being hard on him. I remember her being really strict with my siblings and I growing up. Beating us was the way she handled things. Today it would be called child abuse because she would leave marks and didn't even care that she did. We were to do what she said, no matter what. With no father at home, she was both parents and it was no joke either. I think she was jealous of us when we did get along so she would find ways to break it up. This seemed so crazy to me. I loved her, but thought that she had emotional issues as well.

Before I go on any further, I want it to be known that I loved my mother will all my heart. I loved her more than others could know or could understand. See when you love someone, then you should take the most you can take from them. I tried not to call or visit but I couldn't stay away. I felt sorry for her in so many ways. I was a mother too and it's not easy being a single parent. We never get a handbook or any other material. You go by what you know or what you see. At times, she would not ask if you did something wrong, but would just start by hitting you and ask questions after the fact. There were times when you didn't do anything wrong but she still would hit you.

There were times I would like to just talk with her and be mother and daughter, but it would result in an argument before I knew it. She was just hard to reach no matter what, but again I loved her and prayed there would be a change. I wish my relationship with my mother was better, but she was very bitter at times as well and hard to get close to. My sisters and brother thought I was the pet. Well, I obeyed because I feared her more than being her pet. You love and treat your pets well, but she didn't do the same to me. When I visited her I always bought her something even though she would look at it and the expression on her face told it all, but would say she liked it. It seemed that nothing I did was ever enough.

I had wished her sadness would go away. It hurt me to see her that way, I would ask, "Ma what's the matter?" She wouldn't speak, but she would shake her head. How can you tell that everything is going to be alright when you don't know what's wrong. My siblings knew that she was this way and they also had to deal with it. We each had our own ways of handling it. It was hard for all of us, but it made me not sleep at night, having bad dreams. My siblings never knew how she would tell me that they didn't want anything to do with me. At times I believed it because they never invited me along with them. Or they would say "I thought you didn't want to go", but never asking either. Most times I did feel like I just did not fit in, the way I always dressed up and I didn't feel like what I had on was good enough to wear. So again I felt rejected and would remember her words "they do not want you around". I would ask what did I do and she would laugh. "You know", and I thought to myself I can't think but she again would say, "You know what you did." It was a never-ending puzzle, but I knew I had not done a thing. The hurt I felt they would never understand. But It has not stopped me from just staying away and being happy if it means being without them. There was so much that others said I had said, that it was crazy. The lies were beyond belief, at times, but still told. It's hard to face the facts that this was why I stayed depressed and just didn't care about being a part of their lives. It was too hard and more than I could handle any more. Between my mother and them it was overwhelming. I would of course defend myself. And her favorite words, "O! Come on don't you know what you did?" No matter what I said, it was not the truth, but *they* spoke the truth. I would call and ask,

"What did you tell Ma?" Their answer was, "what you talking about?" This went on for years and it just never got better. This was her way of keeping division between us and believe me it worked. For years, I just wanted to know why a mother would do this. It just didn't make sense to me.

Even when my mother had lung cancer she kept that from us. It was her way of being private and still causing confusion all at the same time. Others knew before her children did, which I still today never understood. She was like that about herself and would tell you about someone else, but I was told a year before she even mentioned it. I was supposed to come to see her that spring, but I had just moved and gotten a new job, so I couldn't leave right then. All she would say is, "I'm sick." I then asked, "What's the matter? Sick from what?" She replied, "O! I guess I will be ok," instead of saying that she had lung cancer and did not have long to live. It took me back to a time when she was in the hospital. She called to the doctor and said she probably would not make it by morning. At the time I was going to Bible College, and the school told me that my mother was very sick. I missed class to go check on her. But as my son and I arrived she was laughing and reading the paper. I was so angry that my son said, "Ma don't get upset." I said to him, "who does that ... calls and says that when they aren't sick at all?" So I thought it was one of these tricks again. But I was wrong, she did have cancer and the way it was told to me I'd rather not go into. But it was a way that could have been done better. I got a call with someone screaming, "go see your mother she is sick." My reply, "why are you screaming?" Talking about it was their way of telling me. Well my baby sister and I went, and my mom looked bad, but she was not humble at all. I thought this might change her. NOT AT ALL. It was sad but I knew it was serious and I just didn't know how short the time would be. From October to December that's all we had. We were not close then, and neither were my sisters and brother. One was saying one thing and the other doing another. But I tried to talk to her and all she wanted to know is if I was going to stay to take care of her. In the beginning I was going to, but I thought to myself that I couldn't do it. That was only because I couldn't handle her or the situation. It was the fact that she was still mean. "What are you looking at?" she said to me, "YES I GOT CANCER, so what." I walked out just full of tears. How could she be so mean even to the nurses? Her way of dealing with it was just not the way that would help her. People with cancer having pleasant attitudes helps with the healing, but for her, that was out of the question. I looked at the situation as, "it's my mother, so let me do what I can." We stayed for a week and then returned home. But in a week she had a decline, so we returned. She was doing well and I stayed at hospital every night. She was very distant, kind to others but rude to me. I still showed unconditional love no matter what she did or said. She was getting weaker and didn't talk. She looked so bad. Before she took that turn she would look for my son, her only grandchild whom she loved dearly. But he didn't get there in time before she died, which was hard on him. Time was going by and she was failing bad. My thoughts were clear. I had given her the cross over to Christ and she received it.

My way of dealing with her death was praying and crying and ask God to keep her close to him. Sad but true, it was a relief not to be tormented any more. But also sad to know that I would not see her anymore. My grandchildren wanted to attend the service, but I wanted them to remember how they last saw her laughing with them and enjoying their company. She was different with them too. They were her joy and my son as well. Doing hospice as a job made it harder to deal with, because it was someone close to me. But she is gone. Some lessons she gave I can keep; they were good ones. These lessons include:

1) do not depend on others to care for you

2) pay your bills

3) do not get too friendly with neighbors

These are things that hold true today and I understand too. My relationship was up and down. There was a time or two where I could laugh and we went shopping, out for lunch and I would say she was good today. I was insecure about myself after hearing how ugly I looked to her…how I would amount to nothing and how I would not be as pretty as her other daughters. "And you are just a glorified butt washer. Who would want you?" These are words I would not ever say to a daughter I had. But that was her way of pulling me down and I thought what she said was true. After a while I thought, "what is the sense of living?", and that I would be happier dead and out of every one's way. I started hating myself, didn't care anymore, drank to feel better, took drugs and men too. I felt maybe this would make the pain I was feeling go away. I was ashamed of how I looked and my feelings were all over the place. I smiled but was dead inside. How was I to go on knowing these feelings were getting the best of me? Never thought she would really feel this way. But I would hear about how she never wanted to go to "that bi—-h's" house (talking about me). And how stupid I was and that I would never make it. All I wanted was her love and attention which she couldn't give at all. She didn't like hugging or you kissing her which I didn't like later in life either. My son would ask me and I would say I do not know. But as time went on I did know I had to keep it to myself. I was too sad to tell him the story that hid grandma didn't like to hug or kiss. I just felt she didn't get that attention either. So how could she give something she never had? How she showed love was a leather coat or a dress or whatever. I'd rather have the words than the clothes. I just knew it was a not what I really needed to survive. I feel that my mother desperately needed to have counseling, but she wouldn't admit to it at all.

I could no longer deal with my depression and the way I felt inside. I just didn't feel good at all, so I did seek counsel and that was what I needed. I didn't realize that they helped me to realize that my mother had issues before we came along. Even years have gone by but back there I received meds to think better and to sleep too. Time went on, my hair got thinner and my face looked a mess because of the meds. But on the inside I felt much better. I was sure that they understood me and knew this was a problem that could be fixed, thank GOD. Some people are ashamed to see someone to seek help, but I knew if I didn't I would have destroyed myself and my son's life as well. To think of killing yourself was something I tried twice and that was a cry for help, but my son's grandmother took a concern and helped me get back to the road of recovery. I was so blessed by that. We are still in touch today, as she is a blessed and kind person. I believed God knew I needed some help along the way. I was hospitalized for a period of time where I was raped mentally as well as physically. It was a road I wish for no one to travel. What kept me alive was my son, knowing he needed me but, he was not confused and troubled as I was. I would call my mother and ask her to visit. She would say that I was crazy and just wanted attention, then hang up. Again, she didn't care and never came to see me at all. I just thought it was so heartless to do. My son needed me as much as I needed him. It was hard being away from him. But his father and grandmother brought him to see me and it was hard to see him leave. I would cry myself to sleep at night, but I had to come to grips with this illness and get better to go home. My mind, my thoughts and my heart needed a fixing beyond a pill. I tried to forget about the rapes that occurred there and how I was the only woman on the male side of the unit. After I was discharged, I still stayed on my meds, and still knew being around my mother was not healthy at all. Sad but true, it was not good at all. I stayed with my son's grandmother, which was a happy and good thing for both of us. I thank God every day for her kindness and love.

I want others to know that abusing your children mentally or physically has effects on their adult lives. It's a life you don't want them to have to go through at all. It's hard enough being a child, then to be harmed, beaten and talked to like a dog. Sorry, but I had to say that because I know it took years for me to be myself. And to feel good about myself as a parent and as a woman too. I learned that she needed help too, but never admitted or wanted it. But it made me feel sorry too that she couldn't see what others knew I needed. It's not a thing like a cold or virus, there is much shame to mental illness today. I had to realize I didn't cause this, but if I let it go what hope would my child have? I'm not as ashamed as used to be, but I see my future better now. I've explained it all to my son so he would never have anyone approach him as I had others approach me when I was growing up, concerning my mother and the things in her life. There are still things today that I couldn't understand and will probably will never do so and maybe that's just how it is. I want my son to be able to come to me without my bitterness getting in the way of us having a good relationship. We have discussed many things and he understands that life can be tough, but it's all about how you deal with it. I have learned so much about what not to do and what needs to be done. It seems hard to believe I meant anything to my mom based on the way she treated me. But I will always know I gave her my best every time we were together. Someone once said to me, "if my mother treated me like that, she would see very little of me." Easier said than done, was my reply to that. It's never easy to walk away from the person who gave you life.

My hope also was to have a relationship with my father, a man I've never met and always wondered why he never came to see about me. My mother would say when I asked, "The best Portage is a dead one." Is that a way to answer a child about her father? But as they say, the streets had nothing good to give or say. There were bad things I heard that he did to me as a young child. That kind of stuff goes on today. It's so hard to believe the person I longed for was a molester too. I had dreams before about things I couldn't understand, but now I know the truth and it's sad to think these situations occurred. I wanted to get ice cream together; have daddy and daughter days. It was never to happen, but to hear years ago that we lived close to each other. When I would hear someone say, "my dad and I went shopping", or "my dad is picking me up", just the thought of him made me cry. And my mother would say that I look just like him, which was not enough information for me. It was like beating a dead horse for her to tell me anything. But I had so many others that played the role of dad. My foster father was quite the dad; pleasant, funny and very loving. I had two male clients from my earlier days of home health that called me daughter and they just did not know how happy that made me. They looked out for me and showed how much they cared for what I was doing for them. It took some of the pain away.

Well, I still didn't feel totally free. But a lady I worked for told me I needed to be delivered, but I didn't know what that was. I looked it up and I was frightened by what I read. But if it meant letting go of it all, I was there. It meant that there were demons that had been released in me. When you are touched as a child, that causes demons to be housed in you. Those experiences and many other things needed to be up rooted out of me. I just didn't know how or when it would take place. One thing I did know in my state of mind was prayer. I asked God to show me who and when. It never happens as we think it will. I went to church knowing that was my place of peace and I loved hearing the word of God. Will this be the day I thought, well time will tell. The sermon was on being free. It seemed as though it was for me. The preacher spoke about how God can take your tears and wash them away and the pain that is wearing you down can go to all the heartache, and will be gone. I could feel myself getting emotional wishing he was talking to me. Then he asked does anyone want to be free from guilt, shame, past hurts, abuse, rape, or anything that is stopping you from having peace. Come now let God deliver you. I sat there scared and was wondering is this my day. Then he came out of the pulpit, looked right at me and said the same words I spoke to myself. "Young lady God is here to heal you. Will you let him today?" I stood up and went to the altar though I felt strange, but I knew I would not be the same when I left there. He said in my ear, "I know your pain. I was once standing where you are now. You will feel God's healing power today just let go and God will take over." I felt this warm feeling come over my body that felt like a shock went through me. Down I went, screaming while others were saying, "just say JESUS." I said it several times over and over then passed out it and stayed down for what seemed like quite some time. After I got up, I felt like I was drunk, but I knew I felt so much better than I did when I came. One of the ladies asked for my number to keep in touch and pray with me. I gave her my phone number and she gave me hers. Oh! What a feeling that came over me! I just never wanted it to go away. I know the devil likes to play for keeps. I no longer wanted to feel unhappy, depressed or just not like myself. I read my word an stayed in the face of God more. The more I did, the more I could feel the spirit winning over my flesh. Deliverance doesn't happen all in one day or night; it was a process for me. And it was letting the demons of depression free and all those other things I did too. It was not just my mother's ways that needed to be lifted from me, but what I did too... the ways of drinking, drugs, men and all others things that attached themselves to me.

I needed to ask God to forgive me for my way of thinking. My attitude had to change in order to serve God. I couldn't have a chip on my shoulder and do whatever pleased me. Someone said to me one day, "how could you have all that in you and act the way you do?" My answer to them was, "you don't know me," but then God responded and said to me, "I do know you and I will strip you of everything if you don't change." As the scripture says, "we can have the gifts without repentance." Right away I apologized to the person I was talking to and today we are closer than ever. I began to tell her my testimony and why I acted the way I did, which was no excuse, but just me being mean. I told her that God doesn't act that way and neither should I. I knew I was wrong and God had given me another chance to get it together and be the woman he had designed me to be. I needed to be Godly sorry for the part I played too. I was angry and had a bad attitude and it had nothing to do with how I would treat others. I repented. I asked God to forgive me and make me whole. Your heart has to be pure before God can forgive you. It means being truly sorry for your actions and ways. A friend asked me how can you have all that in you and act the way you do. The gifts are without repentance. I had to have a "come to JESUS meeting" with myself. But God had told me that day my friend spoke to me, to repent or "I will take all I have put in you away." I went to my friend and told her my testimony and I asked her forgiveness. We are like sisters now. Never think that God will not speak to you about you. If he has chosen you, he will address you in many ways. I knew I didn't go through all that for God not to bring me out. If he brought you to it, he brings you through it. I know by the word that he knew me before he placed me in my mother's womb. He also knew I would do great and marvelous things in my life time. After I went through, I used to think that I never will be the old me. But I can say I'm even better than I was before. I can see my way now and I know who I belong to. I have purpose in life and to serve Jesus is one, to obey is another, and to encourage others. We don't have to look at what we have been through or be bitter when someone asks how did you come through it. This is the hand of God on me since way back when. No more ugly girl. No more, "you are a glorified butt washer." No more tears, but hope for a better tomorrow. Now it's time to be all I can be in God.

I know now that God will never let his spirit dwell in an unclean thing or allow his name to be put to shame. I had some trials, pains and tests, but I have overcome what the devil thought would kill me. I know it was none of me and all of him and I give all glory to my savior, deliverer, way maker and provider. That's why I now walk the walk and talk the talk too. You can only be one way with God. I take this life serious, because I know that he saved me and delivered me for such a time as this.

Never let anyone tell you that God does not care. He does. I know that if he did it for me, why not you? Allow yourself the freedom; he died for you to be free. I know others didn't think I would make it either, Oh! but God did. I want to thank all those who played a part in pushing me on my face, allowing my faith to grow. And those ones that said it is not so. You must trust God even when you can't trace or feel him. The word says that he is closer than a brother and will be there with you when your father or mother forsake you. It took the words of God to bring me full circle and to know his words are true. My prayer is this book will bring life to someone or change their mind about giving up; it's not an option. Dream your dreams, live your life in Christ and see him unfold his purpose and desire in you.

Without my faith, this would not have been possible, but God allows the impossible. And with all I have in me, I want to be used of God in ways that will make him proud. I now know without a doubt that my life was not going anywhere and the only one that could save me was the Lord.

As for my grandchildren, I wanted them to know that without God they will not make it. To be an example to them is very important. We have to live a life that they can follow and receive the blessings of God and his favor. We also have to allow them to know that the truth will always set them free. And to live a lie you will always have to tell one after another to keep up with the first one you told. My grandmother was a missionary, but we never spoke on the things of God or church. But I felt as though she knew the Lord. There were others too that preached and worked in the church. I wish my mother would have sat down and talked to me instead of calling me a holy roller. But she would make sure we went, no matter what. A home with the Lord in it makes a great difference. Now that I have him, it sure is a peace that no one can take away.

I wish my siblings understood me and respected my walk with God. It's what changed me and allowed me to see the mistakes I made and what caused me to be unhappy. I love them and they may never understand what it took for me to be totally free. They didn't at times care or at least they didn't show it . Having a child was hard, and a boy at that, but I did my best.

I always wondered if my mother would have been proud of the woman I have become if she were alive. It's a task every day, but I'd rather have this task than to be as unhappy as I was years ago. I pray that others will realize that even though we all have parents, we don't have to become what they are or were. They may not have known better and I've learned quite a bit of the good and the bad too. It's a spirit that can control you and cause you to miss out on God's rewards for you….the peace, love, hope….everything.

They have no children so they really don't know what the experience is about. My younger sister did help in many ways and it meant more than she will ever know. Took him to Germany and till today they have a relationship that they enjoy talking to each other. Anything I did, they never showed up or asked to be a part of it. I have preached, they never heard me, but one cousin did fly down for one night. But God always has who he wants, even if I wanted them there. I have gotten over asking them to come to anything and they know by now as the saying goes, "it's all good- all God." My journey is not over. I feel God is about to open the heavens and let his glory rain down on their sister like never before. I love you three and want the best God has for you and I pray daily that you are covered, blessed and highly favored. My brother does not keep in touch, it hurts but I have gotten over it. Sometimes I just want to know that I have tried and I don't have to any more. And my other sister, I pray for her spirit and health but pray she finds what truth really is. They both know I have come a long way and that they can say they helped. They showed me that life matters even if I'm not in it with them. Yes it does, but now I matter to those who care and show their true love. And to face the truth is hard, but freeing and healthy.

My son has been through a lot too, he had to see me in my state of not doing well. He had to stay with his other family on his father's side while I was trying to get my mind straight and I thank God for them. They just don't know how much he needed that love. It was hard not to see him and touch or kiss my baby. Yes he was a little boy, and when my life was a mess, I felt bad enough. But to realize it was not all me and that I wanted this feeling to go away so I could come home. As years went on it was hard getting back to being a mother. We made it through rough times and hard ones too. He had to hear things I couldn't explain, but now it's in the past and we are moving on. But I say to any parent that if you know there's a problem, do something about it. Depression is serious and it's no cake walk, but a hell I wish on no one. He survived that and I survived the teenage years with him and that too was rough. But now we are both living our lives, talk a lot and God has blessed me with grands and great grands. We are in a good place, mother and son. He knows what I like and knows what I take serious. I love it when he tells me, "mom you have been a great mother." I always feel if I had not been sick and away from him, maybe things would have been better.

I thank God for him being my prayer partner and my friend too. We are blessed and I know it. We could have been dead in our graves, but God said no. I feel life is good and I won't trade this feeling for anything in this world. I know I can enjoy peace, not just for one day, but a lifetime. To look back on my life and be glad not to look like what I have been through. I thank God for the new friends I have made here in Georgia and how they have become a blessing and a lesson too. My job with hospice work has made me realize life is short; here today gone tomorrow. We never know when he will come, so we must be prepared for his arrival. I enjoyed my church and blessed to have found a place where the Spirit resides and true Love is shown. And my gifts will make room for me. Just don't want this feeling to end living in peace and leaving the rest at Jesus's feet. The more I feel the presence of God, the more I know he is making provisions for my destiny. The closer I get to the Lord; I see my vision coming to pass. I just see things much clearer then before and waiting on God to show me more. When you know it was only the Love of God that made a way for you, you cannot help but praise him. Thanks to my friends and co-workers who were by my side as I would read them my story.

As I go on forward with Bible College and pursuing my writing, I ask God's guidance on all I do. This is my year and I believe it more now than ever. As long as I stay in God's will I can't go wrong and I just pray when I feel things are out of order. I no longer fear that I will not make it. It's not been easy, but I keep going to see what the end will be. And along the way encourage others to pursue their goals and dreams. I never would have thought this dream would come to pass. Well, here it is!

I hope this book will help someone that is hurting from living in the past and not stepping out in faith to see what God can do for them, just as He did for me.

ACKNOWLEDGEMENTS

I dedicate this book to the loving memory of my mother, brother and grandson Carl and to those who have a dream. Don't give up. Trust God and he will make a way.

Thanks to all who supported me as I wrote this book and to Victoria Green Brackins WosLos for believing in me and her kindness and patience also.

www.ingramcontent.com/pod-product-compliance
Lightning Source LLC
Chambersburg PA
CBHW071750040426
42446CB00012B/2517